Original title:
The Endless Journey

Copyright © 2024 Creative Arts Management OÜ
All rights reserved.

Author: George Mercer
ISBN HARDBACK: 978-9916-90-768-9
ISBN PAPERBACK: 978-9916-90-769-6

The Dance of Miles and Moments

Beneath the sky, we wander free,
Each step a breath, a memory.
As distant hills begin to call,
We chase the shadows, never fall.

The sun will rise, then fade away,
Yet in our hearts, the light will stay.
With every turn, a story grows,
In whispered winds, our journey flows.

Endless Reverie of the Road

Paved paths whisper tales of yore,
Each mile a dream, an open door.
Underneath the stars we roam,
The road, a path that feels like home.

Every corner holds a secret bright,
Moments stitched in the fabric of night.
With laughter shared and faces new,
We find ourselves in every view.

Footsteps on an Infinite Path

Footsteps echo on the trail,
In every stride, we set the sail.
Time stretches wide, a canvas bare,
With adventures waiting everywhere.

The horizon blends with our dreams,
In each heartbeat, the world redeems.
With every glance, the future's near,
In endless moments, we persevere.

Whispers of the Road Untraveled

A road less taken, quiet and deep,
Where secrets linger and shadows creep.
Through wildflowers and ancient trees,
We find ourselves on the gentle breeze.

Every twist is a chance to grow,
In whispers of winds, we come to know.
With every step, our spirits rise,
Chasing the dawn, beneath vast skies.

Whispers of the Floating Compass

In twilight's glow, the compass spins,
Whispers of journeys call from within.
Each direction holds a secret tale,
Through shadowed forests, we will sail.

Stars above guide the drifting heart,
Mapping the dreams, where do we start?
With every turn, the world unfolds,
Stories of wonders yet to be told.

Beneath the moon's soft, silvery light,
We chase the horizon, into the night.
With courage found in the quiet space,
We navigate time, in this vast embrace.

Boundless skies and the ocean's roar,
Awaken the spirit to seek and explore.
For whispers of the past softly call,
In the floating compass, we find our all.

Paths Winding Through Eternity

Paths entwine in endless dance,
Each step an echo, a fleeting chance.
Through valleys deep and mountains high,
We wander where dreams and memories lie.

The sunbeams guide through shadowed woods,
In every corner, a heartbeat broods.
Whispers of love, in silence speak,
Through winding trails, we softly seek.

Seasons change, as rivers flow,
In the tapestry of time, we grow.
Each path we tread, a story made,
In the quiet moments, our fears cascade.

At dusk we linger, just you and I,
Beneath the vast and starry sky.
Through eternity's maze, we choose to roam,
Together forever, forever home.

The Map of Unseen Destinies

In shadows dark, the paths unfold,
With stories yet, to be retold.
Each line a whisper, soft and light,
Guiding hearts through endless night.

A compass spins, with fate entwined,
Where dreams merge gently with the blind.
We trace the routes of hopes unspoken,
In the ink of love, our bonds are woven.

Veils of Time and Space

Through curtains thick, the ages blend,
A dance of moments, without end.
Time drips slow, like honey's flow,
In every breath, the echoes grow.

With every step, the worlds align,
The stars above, a sacred sign.
We wander through the drifting haze,
A tapestry of fleeting days.

A Tapestry of Endless Roads

Each path we take, a thread we weave,
In colors bright, we dare believe.
From mountains high to oceans deep,
The journey calls, our hearts to keep.

With every turn, new stories start,
In every beat, a brand new chart.
The roads extend, like dreams in flight,
Guiding us toward the endless light.

Eyes that Wander Beyond

With visions wide, our spirits soar,
To lands unknown, we yearn for more.
Each glance reveals a hidden truth,
In fields of wonder, we find our youth.

The world unfolds beneath our gaze,
A canvas bright with twinkling rays.
In every heart, a spark ignites,
As eyes that wander chase the lights.

Beyond the Last Horizon

Where the sky kisses the sea,
Dreams drift like clouds set free.
Mountains whisper tales in white,
Lost in the glow of fading light.

Stars awaken in the night air,
Guiding hearts that still dare.
Chasing shadows, fleeting and bright,
Beyond the last horizon's sight.

A Dance with Eternity

In the stillness, time unfolds,
A rhythm softly told.
Steps entwined in cosmic grace,
As dreams spin in endless space.

Every heartbeat, a timeless sway,
In the night, we'll lose our way.
A dance where moments intertwine,
With whispers of the divine.

Fragments of an Everlasting Trek

Each step rumbles with the past,
Footprints fade, yet memories last.
Through valleys deep and peaks so high,
We wander where the eagles fly.

Carrying hopes in weathered hands,
Mapping dreams on shifting sands.
Fragments break, yet still they cling,
To every joy that journeys bring.

Sailing Through Timeless Seas

Waves whisper tales of ancient lore,
Sails unfurl to distant shores.
With the stars as our guiding light,
We venture forth into the night.

The ocean's heartbeat calls us near,
Every journey holds its cheer.
Sailing forth on a dream's embrace,
Timeless seas, our sacred space.

Paths Lined with Possibility

Along the winding road we tread,
Dreams like flowers bloom ahead.
Each step whispers hope anew,
A canvas bright in morning dew.

Choices dance upon the breeze,
Open hearts, they long to seize.
With every turn, a chance we find,
To leave the doubts that bind the mind.

Mountains rise and rivers flow,
In the light of what we sow.
A journey born from brave intent,
Paths carved by moments well spent.

Let courage guide our feet so true,
As dreams unfold in skies so blue.
Together, we shall dare to roam,
Discovering the world, our home.

The Flickering Flame of Wanderlust

A flicker in the night ignites,
A yearning heart, a thirst for sights.
With every spark, the spirit soars,
Adventures wait behind closed doors.

Traveling roads both wild and free,
Whispers of the world call me.
To chase horizons far and wide,
As dreams unleash the restless tide.

Through valleys deep and mountains high,
Underneath the painted sky.
The flame within me brightly burns,
With every turn, the heart still yearns.

In distant lands where stars are bright,
I find my peace in wander's light.
A flicker shared, a spark of trust,
In the journey, we all must.

Footfalls in the Mist

Softly drifting, shadows play,
Footfalls lead along the way.
In the hush of morning's grace,
Misty veils begin to trace.

Through the fog, a figure glows,
Time moves slow as the pathway flows.
Every step, a memory calls,
Echoes rise within these walls.

Nature's breath, a gentle sigh,
Whispered secrets drift on by.
In the haze, we find our way,
Lost in thought, yet here we stay.

With the dawn, the world awakes,
In the mist where magic stakes.
Let us wander without fear,
Footfalls soft, our path is near.

Chasing Shadows of Tomorrow

In the twilight, shadows creep,
Chasing dreams that never sleep.
Hope unfurls like wings in flight,
A journey born in fading light.

Every heartbeat paints the day,
In the light of dreams we sway.
Through the dusk, a promise grows,
In the silence, wisdom flows.

Stars appear like distant friends,
Guiding paths that never end.
With every breath, we dare to strive,
Chasing shadows, feeling alive.

Tomorrow waits with arms spread wide,
In the echo of the tides.
Together, we will chase the flame,
As shadows call us by our name.

A Voyage Beyond Time

Sails unfurl to the azure sky,
Whispers of the past drift by.
Waves echo, tales untold,
Hearts of wanderers, brave and bold.

Stars above, a guiding light,
Through the shadowed veil of night.
Each horizon calls my name,
In dreams of lands, I chase the flame.

Time dissolves as I explore,
Mysteries lost on forgotten shores.
A compass made of hope and dreams,
Navigating through cosmic streams.

With every tide, a secret learned,
In the heart, a fire burned.
On this journey, I shall find,
A voyage that transcends all time.

Distant Lights in the Fog

A glow emerges through the haze,
Flickers dim in twilight's gaze.
Voices whisper on the breeze,
Secrets carried with such ease.

In the distance, shadows dance,
Beneath the mist, a fleeting chance.
The horizon bends, a journey starts,
As echoes weave through aching hearts.

Each beacon shines with tales to share,
Guiding souls who wander there.
With gentle hands, the fog unveils,
A tapestry of timeless trails.

Through shrouded paths, I walk anew,
Chasing dreams, both old and true.
In every glimmer, hope ignites,
Distant lights in the thick of nights.

The Flicker of Faraway Lanterns

In the dark, a glow appears,
Dancing lights that calm our fears.
Each lantern burns with whispered dreams,
Guiding hearts through shadowed seams.

Across the fields, they sway and sway,
Leading lost souls, lighting the way.
A flicker here, a flicker there,
Promises of love in the cool night air.

Stories woven with every spark,
Connections made in the silent dark.
Together, we chase the flicker bright,
In the stillness of the night.

As the dawn begins to break,
Fading lights, yet none forsake.
The flicker lingers in our hearts,
A guide to where the journey starts.

Bridges to Tomorrow

Across the river, wide and deep,
A promise made, a bond to keep.
With every step, foundations lay,
Building futures from yesterday.

Wood and stone entwined with dreams,
Echoes of laughter, light that beams.
Hearts united, we traverse,
In flow of time, the universe.

Each bridge a tale, each thread a song,
Carrying dreams where we belong.
Through storms we stand, through trials we rise,
With hope as bright as the morning skies.

Together we journey, hand in hand,
Creating paths across this land.
With every step, we lay the ground,
For bridges to tomorrow, safe and sound.

Fragments of Time's Canvas

Gentle strokes on faded dreams,
Colors blur in silent screams.
Moments caught in fleeting hues,
Whispers lost, we dare to choose.

In shadows cast by yesterday,
Memories weave and drift away.
Each thread a story, soft and bright,
Blinking stars in the hush of night.

Seasons change and palettes fade,
Yet the heart, it won't evade.
Painting life in shades of grace,
Finding beauty in its trace.

A canvas speaks of joys and pains,
Fragments held, through love's refrains.
Hold them close, let colors run,
For in these pieces, we have won.

Raindrops on a Traveler's Soul

Pitter-patter on weary roads,
Each raindrop bears a story's load.
Windswept paths and skies of gray,
Travelers pause, then fade away.

A rhythm soft, a heart's lament,
In every drop, a soul is spent.
Through puddles deep, reflections swim,
Lost in dreams that echo dim.

Rivers form from tears untold,
Life's journeys brave, yet still so bold.
Wet footprints mark where futures tread,
In every storm, a moment's thread.

Raindrops fall like clumsy notes,
In harmony, their silence floats.
Each splash a chance, a fleeting role,
A reminder soft—revive the soul.

A Symphony of Unfinished Dialogues

Words hang thick in heavy air,
Softly spoken, a silent prayer.
Conversations left to sigh,
Notes unsung, beneath the sky.

Voices echo from the past,
Fragments shared but never cast.
Like open books with pages torn,
Stories live, both lost and worn.

Each pause a rhythm, each breath a beat,
A dance of thoughts that never meet.
In the silence, truths may dwell,
Unfinished tales, a living spell.

Let us linger on the brink,
In between the words we think.
For in the space, a promise gleams,
A symphony of hidden dreams.

Paths Woven with Stardust

In twilight's glow, where dreams ignite,
Paths entwine in soft moonlight.
Footsteps trace the arc of fate,
Woven threads, we navigate.

Each twist and turn a story spun,
Guided gently by the sun.
Stardust whispers in the breeze,
Carrying hopes with graceful ease.

Galaxies in every sigh,
Journeys reached beneath the sky.
With every star, a wish is cast,
As we walk, we hold the past.

Together here, our paths align,
Interwoven, yours and mine.
In this dance of cosmic grace,
We find our home in time and space.

A Map without Corners

In a world of lines that meet,
Travelers find their own beat.
With no edges to confine,
Journeys start where stars align.

Paths unwritten call the brave,
Hearts that wander, dreams to stave.
Through the wild, in ink so bold,
Stories long and yet untold.

Guided by the compass inside,
No need for maps, just trust the ride.
Beyond the borders, freedom swells,
In whispered tales, adventure dwells.

Every twist may seem a maze,
But in each turn, the spirit plays.
Together in this vast expanse,
Life is but a daring dance.

Reflections on a Dusty Trail

Beneath the sun, the earth is warm,
Footprints dance, a silent charm.
Memories linger in the air,
Whispers of those who ventured there.

Old oaks stand, their shadows cast,
Echoes of laughter in the past.
Dust spins soft in twilight's glow,
The trail reveals what we may know.

Each step tells a story true,
In every bend, a world anew.
The rustling leaves, the call of night,
Guide lost souls toward the light.

As stars emerge in velvet skies,
Dreams awaken, shadows rise.
On this trail, we hear the refrain,
Life's melody, like falling rain.

The Light beyond the Horizon

A glimmer breaks the edge of night,
Promises whispered, soft and bright.
Hope's sweet glow ignites the day,
Leading us on, come what may.

Waves of color paint the skies,
In every hue, a new surprise.
We chase the dawn, our spirits high,
With wings of faith, we learn to fly.

Beyond the hills, the future waits,
Unlocking dreams behind the gates.
With open hearts, we gather light,
Stepping boldly into the bright.

In every moment, sparks ignite,
A tapestry of love and sight.
The horizon beckons, calling clear,
To embrace the journey we hold dear.

Forests of Forgotten Paths

In a thicket where shadows sneak,
Whispers of time both soft and weak.
Old trails fade where silence sways,
Lost in the rhythm of ancient days.

Mossy stones and twisted trees,
Under the branches, a gentle breeze.
Echoes linger of those who roamed,
In this wild, the heart finds home.

Sunlight dapples the forest floor,
Each step a journey to explore.
Lost legends hide in the green,
In every nook, secrets unseen.

Among the roots, a story brews,
With every glance, the past imbues.
Forests deep, where memories dwell,
Guardians of dreams they hold so well.

Footprints in the Cosmic Sand

In the silence where stars gleam,
Footprints mark the cosmic stream.
Winds of time softly weave,
Stories of those who believe.

Galaxies whisper secrets old,
In the sand, dreams are told.
Each mark a tale of the bold,
In the universe, treasures unfold.

Beneath the dark, hearts ignite,
With each step, we chase the light.
Footprints linger, shimmering bright,
Guiding souls through the night.

In this vast, endless expanse,
We dance the stars in a cosmic trance.
Footprints faded, yet still we roam,
In the universe, we find our home.

The Journey of Every Star

Born from dust in the dark night,
Each star holds a flickering light.
Through eons, they rise and fall,
In the silence, we heed their call.

Travelers on a journey grand,
Spanning space, a timeless band.
Guiding wanderers through the sky,
Each has a tale, no need to pry.

From the cradle of a bright nebula,
To the end, a stellar bulla.
Each journey paints the sky's face,
In their glow, we find our place.

So look above, let dreams take flight,
Follow the path of starlit light.
For in each journey, great and far,
Lives the story of every star.

Streams of Hope

In the valley where rivers flow,
Whispers of dreams begin to grow.
Clear waters reflecting hearts true,
Carrying wishes through and through.

Beneath the shade of ancient trees,
Hope dances gently with the breeze.
Every ripple tells a tale,
Of love that lasts, will not pale.

As the sun paints the evening sky,
Streams shimmer under the watchful eye.
Each drop a promise, a tender plea,
Woven together, wild and free.

In the currents where spirits meet,
Hope ignites in every heartbeat.
Flowing onward, forever bound,
In streams of hope, life is found.

Eyes Set on an Eternal Sky

Beneath a canopy of stars,
Dreamers gaze from near and far.
With each flicker, visions bloom,
In silence, the universe looms.

Hearts open wide, like wings set free,
Chasing wonders, just to be.
Eyes that sparkle, souls on fire,
Reaching up, we climb higher.

Every constellation tells a tale,
Of journeys where the brave prevail.
In the night, our spirits fly,
With eyes set on an eternal sky.

As dawn breaks, the stars may fade,
But in our hearts, the dreams are laid.
Eyes still shining, hope will guide,
Forever drawn to the cosmic tide.

Scattered Stars on the Journey

Beneath the vast and endless night,
Scattered stars ignite the flight.
Each twinkle holds a whispered dream,
Guiding hearts, so it would seem.

Through the silence, echoes call,
In shadows deep, we rise or fall.
Every step a tale untold,
In the cosmos, brave and bold.

Paths entwined in celestial glow,
Waves of fate in cosmic flow.
In the galaxy's warm embrace,
We wander, seeking our own place.

As stardust weaves our story bright,
Together, we traverse the night.
In every moment, a spark appears,
Scattered stars, through hopes and fears.

A Saga of Eternal Suspense

In the heart of shadows deep,
Secrets wake, and silence weep.
Each moment births a brand-new tale,
In the silence, ghosts prevail.

Threads of fate begin to weave,
In the dusk, we laugh, we grieve.
A whisper caught, a fleeting glance,
In the web, we find our chance.

Time eludes, the clock stands still,
Promises made, yet unfulfilled.
Suspense lingers, tension grows,
In the dark, the true self shows.

Every heartbeat is a sign,
With every breath, fate aligns.
In this saga, shadows dance,
Through tangled lives, we take our stance.

Unraveled Threads of Destiny

With fingers tracing fate's soft weave,
Unraveled threads, we dare believe.
In a tapestry of dreams once tight,
We find our paths in fading light.

Choices made in fleeting time,
Each moment dances, pure as rhyme.
Stitched with hopes and whispered fears,
Destiny calls through laughter, tears.

Colors bleed, intentions shift,
In the fabric, each thread a gift.
Life unfolds, both bright and dim,
In the chaos, we learn to swim.

So let us cherish each small thread,
And weave a future, not just dread.
For in the strands of what we find,
Love and purpose intertwine.

Sojourns in the Realm of Forever

In the mystic realm where dreams reside,
Sojourns hum beneath the tide.
Timeless echoes guide our feet,
In the stillness, we feel complete.

Moments linger like fragrant blooms,
Filling hearts, dispelling glooms.
Every whisper, a gentle breeze,
In the realm, we find our ease.

Paths unfolding in twilight's grace,
A dance of shadows, an endless space.
In the glow of stars above,
We wander forth, we seek our love.

Forever waits with open arms,
Embracing all our dreams and charms.
In the journey through time's embrace,
We find our home, our sacred place.

Rivers of Memory Flowing

In quiet streams, old echoes play,
Fragments of laughter, faded each day.
Whispers of dreams, on currents they glide,
Winding through time, where shadows abide.

Reflections dance on the water's face,
Tales of the heart, a soft embrace.
In every ripple, a story is told,
Of love and of loss, of young and of old.

As twilight wraps its gentle shawl,
We gather the moments, both big and small.
In rivers of memory, we find our way,
Flowing onward, forever to stay.

In Search of the Lost Compass

Beneath the stars, I roam the night,
Seeking direction, lost in the light.
The winds they whisper, the shadows they tease,
A compass of dreams, caught in the breeze.

Paths intertwined, yet none feel true,
Each step I take, I'm lost anew.
Searching the silence, yearning for signs,
In the heart's wild corners, where hope still shines.

The world keeps spinning, a dizzying dance,
Hoping to stumble upon a chance.
Each moment a clue, in the vast unknown,
To find my way home, to where I belong.

The Dance of the Wandering Sky

Above the earth, the heavens twirl,
As clouds embrace and winds unfurl.
Stars like dancers, they spin and glide,
In the vastness where dreams reside.

The moon dips low, a silken sway,
Casting soft light on night's ballet.
Comets trail tales of journeys begun,
In the boundless stage, where nothing's undone.

A symphony plays, the cosmos hums,
A tapestry woven, as starlight comes.
In the dance of the sky, my spirit finds,
The rhythm of life, where love unwinds.

A Map Made of Wishes

On parchment of dreams, I draw my way,
With ink of hope, I long to stay.
Each wish a landmark, a guiding star,
Leading my heart to where fortunes are.

Mountains of courage, rivers of grace,
I chart my course to a kinder place.
With every stroke, new paths align,
In the mosaic of fate, where stars entwine.

A compass of faith, each point a goal,
In the map made of wishes, I find my role.
With courage to follow and dreams to unfurl,
I navigate life, a wondrous world.

The Quest that Knows No End

In fields of whispers, seekers roam,
With hearts ablaze for the unknown.
Each step a tale, each breath a chance,
To chase the light where shadows dance.

Mountains rise with secrets deep,
Through valleys vast, our dreams we'll keep.
The horizon calls, a siren's song,
Inviting souls to journey long.

Stars above, a map of fate,
Guide us forth, we won't be late.
In every turn, a lesson found,
The quest persists, with joy unbound.

Together we sail through night and day,
For every lost, there's hope to sway.
With every heartbeat, spirits blend,
In this grand quest that knows no end.

Wandering Souls and Celestial Paths

In starlit realms where spirits glide,
Wandering souls, side by side.
They trace the paths of time and space,
In endless chase for hope's embrace.

With whispers soft, the cosmos sings,
Of journeys vast and cherished things.
Each echo hears a silent plea,
To wander on, forever free.

Galaxies spin, a cosmic dance,
In fleeting moments, hearts will prance.
Through shadows thick, we find our way,
In twilight hues, the night turns gray.

A tapestry of dreams we weave,
In every thread, we dare believe.
For wandering souls know no defeat,
In celestial paths, our hearts will meet.

Shadows on the Perpetual Way

Beneath the arch of midnight skies,
Shadows linger, truth belies.
They whisper tales of days long gone,
On the pathways where dreams are drawn.

Each footstep echoes through the dark,
In silent woods, they leave a mark.
A gentle breeze begins to sway,
As shadows dance upon the way.

With lantern light to guide our sight,
We journey forth, hearts shining bright.
In every bend, a fear takes flight,
Yet courage blooms in deep of night.

So onward still, we forge ahead,
Through shadows cast, we fight our dread.
For on this road, we learn to play,
And find ourstrength on the perpetual way.

The Compass of Unending Dreams

A compass spins with fervent grace,
Pointing to realms where dreams embrace.
In every glance, a vision stirs,
A call to wander, life prefers.

With every sigh, we seek the dawn,
Through twilight's path, we'll carry on.
For in the heart, the compass lies,
A beacon bright in the deepest skies.

As rivers flow and mountains breathe,
In every hope, new worlds conceive.
The dreams we chase will not be tamed,
In whispered nights, our hearts are claimed.

With every turn, a story flows,
In unending dreams, our spirit grows.
For life's great journey will not cease,
The compass spins, leading to peace.

Wandering in a Dreamscape

In twilight's glow, I drift away,
Through misty paths where shadows play.
Whispers of thoughts, both soft and light,
Guide me to realms of endless night.

Colors swirl in a mystic dance,
Each step I take, a fleeting chance.
I touch the sky, taste the stars,
Lost in the magic, forgetting scars.

A river flows with memories dim,
Beneath the moon, the lights grow slim.
Floating on dreams, I laugh and sigh,
In this vast world, I learn to fly.

When morning comes, I gently wake,
With echoes of all that I could make.
Yet in my heart, I hold it tight,
The dreamscape whispers, "You'll be alright."

The Rhythm of Change

Leaves flutter down, a golden hue,
Time moves softly, with every view.
A clock ticks on, the seasons shift,
Life's sweet dance, a precious gift.

Moments unfold, like petals bloom,
Chasing away shadows of gloom.
Each heartbeat sings a different song,
A melody where we all belong.

Waves crash softly upon the shore,
Reminding us of what's in store.
With every dawn, new colors rise,
Transforming dreams beneath the skies.

So let us sway with each new beat,
Embrace the change, feel the heat.
For life's a rhythm, wild and free,
A dance of souls, in harmony.

Timeless Footprints

On softest sands, our paths we trace,
In each grain, a story's place.
Footprints echo of days gone by,
Beneath the vast and open sky.

Through winding roads and starlit nights,
We chase the dreams, we seek the lights.
Every step holds a whispered vow,
To cherish the present, here and now.

In meadows green and mountains high,
We leave our marks as time floats by.
With every laugh and every tear,
Our journey sings, so sweet, so dear.

When years have passed, and tales are told,
In memory's warmth, we'll never grow old.
For footprints fade, yet love remains,
In the heart's embrace, where joy sustains.

Chasing Shadows on Sunlit Streets

Beneath the sun, where shadows play,
We wander through the light of day.
Laughter spills from every lane,
A dance of joy, forget the pain.

The pavement sparkles, stories told,
In every crack, there's warmth and gold.
We race with dreams through fragrant air,
A tapestry woven with care.

With every turn, new faces shine,
A fleeting glimpse, the heart aligns.
Chasing shadows, we never tire,
In the pulse of life, we feel desire.

As twilight falls, the colors blend,
In the magic realm where spirits mend.
We'll keep on dancing, side by side,
Chasing shadows, where love abides.

Whispers of an Infinite Path

In shadows where the secrets lie,
Soft murmurs call in the night sky.
Each step a tale that winds and weaves,
In silence held by autumn leaves.

A dance of dreams in twilight glow,
Each heartbeat whispers where to go.
The path unfolds, a gentle sway,
Guiding souls who lost their way.

Stars above, they flicker bright,
Illuminating the silent flight.
With every turn, horizons blend,
Forever drawn, we will ascend.

Beneath the sky, a canvas wide,
We walk together, side by side.
In echoes of the past we find,
The infinite path that binds the mind.

Uncharted Horizons

A sea of dreams stretches afar,
Beneath the sun, beneath the star.
Waves of hope crash on the shore,
Carving paths that beg for more.

In whispered winds, new tales arise,
Adventurers chase the endless skies.
With hearts ablaze, they dare to roam,
Across the wild, they make their home.

Mountains rise with stories grand,
Each peak a question, each ridge a hand.
We search for truths in the unknown,
In every step, we find our own.

With every dawn, a canvas fresh,
Uncharted dreams in every flesh.
Together we'll explore wide seas,
In unison, with gentle ease.

Footsteps on an Eternal Road

Footsteps echo on the ancient stone,
A journey shared, never alone.
Each mark we leave—a tale of grace,
In endless time, we find our place.

Through valleys deep and mountains high,
Beneath the vast and watchful sky.
We walk the line of years gone past,
In every moment, shadows cast.

The road unfolds, a ribbon bright,
With every turn, we chase the light.
In laughter shared, in tears we find,
An eternal bond that's intertwined.

With every heartbeat, stories blend,
In footfalls strong, our hopes ascend.
Together we forge paths untold,
With whispered dreams, our lives unfold.

Boundless Voyage

Set sail upon the ocean wide,
With open hearts, we'll not divide.
The horizon calls with sweet embrace,
In every wave, we find our place.

Stars will guide us through the night,
In darkness deep, we'll search for light.
Every tide brings whispers near,
Beneath the sky, we shed our fear.

Each island holds a story rare,
A treasure found, a breath of air.
In the dance of waves, we lose and find,
A boundless journey of heart and mind.

Together we chase the fading sun,
In every heartbeat, we are one.
The voyage stretches, ever bold,
In dreams of boundless tales retold.

Horizon's Embrace

The sun dips low, a fiery glow,
Where sea and sky gently meet,
A canvas brushed with gold and rose,
Whispers of dreams in the heat.

Waves caress the sandy shore,
Secrets held in salty spray,
Each crest brings stories of yore,
As daylight fades into gray.

Clouds dance in the fading light,
Casting shadows, soft and light,
The horizon stretches far and wide,
A promise kept in endless tide.

And as the stars emerge above,
They twinkle like a lover's gaze,
In the hush of twilight's embrace,
Hope rekindles in the night's maze.

Where Stars Whisper Secrets

Beneath a dome of twinkling light,
Silent tales in shadows play,
Constellations' ancient flight,
Guide the lost who drift away.

Each star a wish, a prayer sent forth,
Hopes entwined in cosmic dance,
In the silence, dreams give birth,
To paths unseen, a fleeting glance.

Galaxies spin in endless night,
A symphony of cosmic lore,
Where silence reigns and hearts take flight,
In the depths of the universe's core.

Listen closely, hear them call,
The echoes of our long-lost dreams,
A tapestry of light weaves all,
In the starry sky, everything gleams.

Beyond the Distant Shore

Waves crash softly, a gentle roar,
Secrets hidden in the foam,
Journeys wait on the distant shore,
Where hearts can wander, and roam.

Each tide brings change, a new embrace,
Echoes of laughter, whispers of sighs,
In the salt-kissed air, we find our place,
Underneath the endless skies.

Seagulls cry as the day unfolds,
A promise written in the sand,
Together we chase what the ocean holds,
Hand in hand, we dare to stand.

With each sunset painting the sky,
Dreams set sail on twilight's breeze,
Beyond the waves, our spirits fly,
In the vastness, we find peace.

Echoes of Wandering Souls

In twilight's glow, the spirits roam,
Whispers soft on the evening air,
Each echo tells of a far-off home,
A tale of longing, of despair.

Through ancient woods where shadows play,
Ghostly figures dance and spin,
Memories linger, never to stray,
Their melody entwined within.

As the moon weaves silver light,
Secrets of time drift past our sight,
Wandering souls, both young and old,
Carry stories yet untold.

So listen close, for in the night,
The echoes call to brave the dark,
In every shadow, there is light,
A spark of life, a timeless mark.

Through the Unseen Corridors

In shadows deep, where whispers lie,
Footsteps tread on dreams that sigh.
Fragments of light, a gentle gleam,
Guide us softly, like a dream.

Walls breathe stories, etched in time,
Silent echoes, a distant chime.
With every turn, we pause and see,
The unseen paths that set us free.

Beyond the veil, where secrets dwell,
Curiosity casts its spell.
Through twisted halls and faded door,
We find the truth that we explore.

Together we wander, hand in hand,
Through corridors of a forgotten land.
In the silence, we hear a call,
Through the unseen, we break the wall.

The Echo of Distant Horizons

Beneath the sky where dreams take flight,
Horizons stretch, a wondrous sight.
Whispers travel on the breeze,
Carrying tales from the seas.

Mountains loom, their peaks aglow,
Embracing the sunset's warm flow.
With every dusk, the stars appear,
Echoes of hopes and dreams held dear.

Across the fields where shadows play,
Memories linger, come what may.
With every heartbeat, a distant call,
The echo of horizons, embracing all.

We chase the sun, we run the race,
Seeking wonders, a new embrace.
In every moment, the world unfolds,
The echo of distant tales retold.

A River that Never Rests

A river flows through time and space,
With gentle whispers, it keeps pace.
Over stones and under skies,
It carries dreams, it softly sighs.

Through valleys deep, it winds its way,
Reflecting colors of night and day.
In every ripple, secrets hide,
Life's stories carried on the tide.

It dances round the ancient trees,
And bends with grace in the soft breeze.
A journey endless, a song unchained,
A river's heart, forever sustained.

Like thoughts that wander, never still,
It carves the earth with patience and will.
In every drop, a universe rests,
A river flows, and it never rests.

All Roads Lead to Mystery

Paths entwine beneath the stars,
With every step, we chase our scars.
A labyrinth of dreams takes form,
In every shadow, a truth is born.

Footprints drift like whispered lore,
Guiding us to an ancient door.
With open hearts, we seek and find,
The mystery that haunts the mind.

In every turn, a choice awaits,
Uncharted destinies, tempting fates.
Each moment blends the known and new,
All roads lead where the soul breaks through.

In the silence, we hear the song,
Of journeys traveled, forever long.
Together we wander through the night,
For all roads lead to endless light.

Chasing Flickers of Infinity

In the twilight's gentle embrace,
Stars whisper secrets of grace.
Moments flicker, then they fade,
In endless night, dreams are laid.

Chasing shadows, lost in time,
We dance beneath the silver chime.
Each heartbeat echoes cosmic song,
In this vastness, we belong.

Silent wishes scatter wide,
As galaxies in silence glide.
Through the dark, we find our way,
Chasing flickers, night turns day.

And when the dawn begins to break,
With every choice, a new path takes.
Fleeting moments guide our flight,
Chasing wonders, pure delight.

Rivers Flowing into Tomorrow

Rivers carve their ancient trails,
Secrets whispered in the gales.
Each curve a story, each bend a tale,
Flowing onward, never pale.

Time moves like water, swift and fast,
Carrying dreams from future and past.
In its depths, reflections gleam,
Rivers of thought, a waking dream.

Underneath the bridge of night,
Stars above, a guiding light.
As currents twist, new paths are born,
Rivers flowing, never torn.

With every drop, the journey grows,
Into tomorrow, the river flows.
A dance of time, a fluid grace,
In the embrace of nature's face.

Endless Shadows at Dusk

Beneath the trees, the shadows play,
As dusk descends, it takes the day.
Whispers linger on the breeze,
In twilight's hush, the heart finds peace.

Endless echoes softly call,
In the fading light, they gently fall.
Caught between what's lost and found,
In shadows deep, our dreams abound.

Colors blend, a canvas wide,
As night approaches, we confide.
In the silence, truth revives,
Endless shadows as life thrives.

Hold on tight, the night will pass,
But in its arms, we'll find our glass.
Reflection holds what once was true,
In endless shadows, dreams renew.

The Tapestry of Infinite Paths

Threads of fate weave through the night,
Colors dancing, hearts alight.
Each strand holds a dream untold,
In this tapestry of gold.

Infinite paths beneath our feet,
Choices linger, bittersweet.
A journey crafted stitch by stitch,
Life unfolds, a wondrous niche.

In the weft and warp of time,
Moments shimmer, clear as rhyme.
Every knot, a memory calls,
In this fabric, the spirit sprawls.

Hold the threads, embrace the weave,
For in this art, we learn to believe.
The tapestry stretches far and wide,
Infinite paths, our dreams abide.

The Wayfarer's Unbroken Saga

With a pack upon my back, I roam,
Each step a tale, a call to home.
The stars above whisper their lore,
Guiding me onward, forevermore.

Paths wind through valleys deep and wide,
Each moment cherished, none will hide.
The mountains sing, the rivers flow,
In every gust, the sweet winds blow.

With every stranger, stories weave,
In shared laughter, hearts believe.
Each sunset paints a vibrant scene,
In the journey, life is keen.

Through storm and calm, I find my way,
In nature's arms, I choose to stay.
The road unknowing, yet I am free,
In every moment, I choose to be.

Timeless Echoes of Solitude

In quiet corners of the mind,
Where shadows dance, peace we find.
Whispers linger, soft and clear,
A solitude that draws us near.

The echoing silence tells a tale,
Of countless thoughts, frail and pale.
Yet in stillness, wisdom springs,
The heart takes flight on unseen wings.

Beneath the stars, in night's embrace,
We find ourselves in empty space.
Reflections stir, like rippling streams,
In solitude, we chase our dreams.

Embracing quiet, fears take flight,
In gentle shadows, we find delight.
With every breath, we start anew,
In timeless echoes, our spirits grew.

The Unseen Journey of Hearts

In the depths of silence, hearts entwine,
A thread unbroken, a bond divine.
Beyond the surface, love does grow,
In gentle pulses, we come to know.

Through trials faced and battles won,
In every moment, two become one.
Eyes meet softly, stories unfold,
In warmth of touch, our truths are told.

The journey's path may twist and turn,
Yet in each other, we brightly burn.
Unseen by many, our love shines bright,
Guiding us through the darkest night.

With whispered promises, we stand tall,
In the unseen journey, we'll never fall.
Hearts aligned, a sacred art,
Together always, never apart.

This Never-Ending Spiral

Life unfolds in circles drawn,
Each twist a lesson, a new dawn.
Embracing change, we rise and fall,
In this spiral dance, we heed the call.

With every turn, we crave the light,
In shadows deep, we search for sight.
The past encircles, yet we break free,
In every cycle, we learn to see.

Moments blend as seasons change,
In familiar realms, we feel so strange.
Yet in the spiral, hope ignites,
A flame that flickers, a beacon bright.

Though paths may twist and curves may bend,
We journey on, with no clear end.
In this endless circle, life imparts,
A tapestry woven within our hearts.

Trails of Forgotten Dreams

Whispers of a twilight breeze,
Echoes of what used to be.
Shadows dance in silent trees,
Chasing thoughts that wander free.

Footprints on a fallen leaf,
Stories told with every sigh.
Moments lost to time's belief,
Fragments of a lullaby.

Ghosts of laughter fill the air,
Flickering in fading light.
Hopes once bright, now threadbare,
Chasing stars that lost their flight.

Yet in the heart, they linger on,
Softly stitched with golden seams.
Though the roads they walk are gone,
They live on in quiet dreams.

Celestial Beacons in the Dark

Stars like candles in the night,
Guiding souls with gentle glow.
Each one holds a tale in flight,
In their dance, the cosmos flow.

Moonlight spills on silver seas,
Whispers of a cosmic song.
Waves of light like whispered pleas,
In the vastness, we belong.

Nebulas in colors bright,
Painting skies with cosmic dust.
A universe both bold and slight,
In the dark, we place our trust.

Dreams unfold beneath the stars,
Hope ignites with every spark.
In the vastness, love is ours,
Celestial beacons in the dark.

Markers in the Sand

Footprints trail along the shore,
Tales of journeys left behind.
Waves wash in, then out once more,
Whispers of the sea, so kind.

Shells collected, each a prize,
Echoes of the ocean's song.
Sunrise paints the morning skies,
In this place, we all belong.

Time erases with each tide,
Yet memories are carved in hearts.
Though the currents swiftly glide,
Love remains as time departs.

Markers in the sand we leave,
Stories etched in grains of gold.
Though the wind may choose to weave,
Every tale will still be told.

Between Here and Forever

Moments caught in endless flow,
Time suspended in a dream.
What we feel, we deeply know,
Life is more than what it seems.

Between the heartbeat, love ignites,
Whispered promises take flight.
In the dusk, we chase the lights,
Finding solace in the night.

Every breath, a step we take,
Navigating through the haze.
In the tides, our hearts awake,
In between, we find our ways.

Here, the past and future blend,
A tapestry of lost and found.
In this space, our souls transcend,
Between here and forever, bound.

The Uncharted Symphony

In twilight's hush, the echoes bloom,
Notes of dusk adorn the room.
Whispers call from realms unknown,
A melody of hearts overgrown.

Each chord a story to unfold,
In the silence, truths are told.
Waves of sound, a gentle tide,
In every note, our dreams abide.

The stars compose a grand refrain,
While shadows dance, they feel no pain.
An orchestra of hope and fear,
The uncharted symphony draws near.

Together we weave, with each new song,
In this embrace, we all belong.
With every breath, we play our part,
An unspoken song from the heart.

Sands Through the Hourglass

Grains of time slip quietly down,
Marking moments, our lives renown.
Each second, a treasure, brief and bright,
Woven into the fabric of night.

With every fall, memories fade,
In the dance of time, we are made.
Sands of gold, in shadows cast,
A fleeting whisper of the past.

Ticking clocks remind us all,
Of laughter shared, and silent calls.
Through the glass, we yearn and plead,
For time to linger, for hearts to heed.

Yet in each grain, a story lies,
Of dreams fulfilled and tender sighs.
So let us cherish every glance,
In life's hourglass, there's always a chance.

Whirling Dreams of Distant Lands

In twilight skies, vast dreams take flight,
With whispers soft, they chase the night.
Over mountains, and seas so grand,
They swirl and swirl, a magic band.

Each vision sparkles, a fleeting light,
Guiding souls in the gentle night.
Far-off places beckon near,
In whirling dreams, we shed our fear.

From desert sands to snowy peaks,
In every heart, a longing speaks.
The pulse of lands we've never trod,
In dreams we wander, we feel the God.

Let us embrace this wondrous flight,
With open hearts, we'll chase the light.
For in the dance of time and space,
Each dream reveals a sacred place.

A Journey Through the Unseen

Beneath the veil, where shadows play,
We wander paths that dreamers lay.
In whispers soft, the world unfolds,
A journey told, yet never bold.

Through hidden doors and flickering lights,
We chase the magic of endless nights.
Each turn a tale, each step a chance,
In this unseen world, we dare to dance.

Voices echo with secrets deep,
In realms of dreams, where visions leap.
Hand in hand, we brave the unknown,
In this journey, we've brightly grown.

So let us wander, hearts entwined,
In the unseen, true peace we'll find.
For in the quiet, we hear the call,
A journey through the unseen—a gift for all.

The Ceaseless Quest

In shadows deep, we seek the light,
A flicker bright in endless night.
With every step, a tale unfolds,
A thousand dreams in silence told.

The whispered winds call out our names,
Through whispered woods, we play our games.
Each path we tread, a chance to find,
The hidden truths that haunt the mind.

Beyond the hills, where rivers flow,
Our spirits rise, and courage grows.
In every heart, a fire burns,
The ceaseless quest, the world returns.

In search of stars, we chase the dawn,
With every dusk, a hope reborn.
Together bound, our fate entwined,
The journey's end, we seek to find.

Songs of the Pathless Travelers

With weary feet on roads unknown,
The songs we sing, forever sown.
In every note, a story flows,
Of distant lands where wanderers go.

We dance beneath the silver moon,
A symphony of hearts in tune.
Through valleys wide and mountains high,
Our spirits soar, our dreams will fly.

Each melody a breath of fate,
In harmony, we celebrate.
The pathless ways, our souls ignite,
A journey shared, a pure delight.

Through whispered winds, our songs resound,
In every beat, true love is found.
The road ahead calls out our names,
In sacred joy, we'll fan the flames.

Shadows of the Eternal Voyage

In drifting dreams, we sail the night,
With every wave, we chase the light.
The shadows dance, with stories old,
Their whispered truths, a treasure gold.

Across the seas of time we roam,
In search of hearth, we find our home.
The stars above our compass guide,
In every heartbeat, love implied.

The winds of fate, they shift and swell,
In every sigh, a wish to tell.
The eternal voyage, vast and wide,
With open hearts, we'll turn the tide.

Through darkest storms, our spirits stay,
Together strong, we find our way.
In shadows deep, we rise, we soar,
The eternal dreams forevermore.

When the Heart Roams Wild

When twilight falls, the heart takes flight,
In whispered realms, it finds the light.
With every breath, a spark ignites,
The world's embrace in endless nights.

Through forests deep, where secrets hide,
The wilds within, our souls abide.
In passion's dance, we lose our way,
To find the truth within the sway.

With untamed winds, our spirits free,
In every beat, a symphony.
When wandering hearts break every chain,
In love's pure fire, we rise again.

The wild unknown, a lover's call,
Where echoes linger, we shall fall.
In open skies, our dreams run wild,
The heart unbound, forever styled.

Echoes of the Unseen Trail

In the whispers of the breeze,
Secrets linger, softly tease.
Footsteps trace a hidden way,
Where shadows dance and shadows play.

Beneath the canopy's embrace,
Nature holds a sacred space.
Every rustle, every sound,
Tells a tale of night unbound.

Paths entwined with ancient lore,
Lead to realms we can explore.
Each turn taken, every mile,
Fuels the heart with nature's smile.

So wander on with open eyes,
For echoes hide in every sigh.
On unseen trails, the journey's made,
In quiet moments, dreams won't fade.

Odyssey of a Thousand Tomorrows

Waves of time rush to the shore,
Each tomorrow waits, holds more.
A canvas vast, of bright and gray,
Future threads weave through today.

Stars align in skies so wide,
Guiding dreams on a hopeful tide.
With courage, hearts will break the mold,
In every story, courage told.

Footsteps falter, yet they soar,
From mountain high to ocean floor.
The quest is long, the path is steep,
But within each laugh, our spirits leap.

So let the dawns unfold anew,
With grace, we chase skies painted blue.
In this odyssey, together we go,
Crafting tales of joy and woe.

Roads that Never Converge

Two paths diverge, a silent choice,
Echoes linger, yet no voice.
Separate ways, the journey starts,
Each with dreams, and beating hearts.

Wanderers tread on different skies,
Chasing sunsets, under distant sighs.
Though miles apart, they feel the pull,
Of memories shared, forever full.

Time unfolds like petals fair,
Yet fondness thrives in open air.
The distance grows, but love transcends,
On roads like rivers, that twist and bend.

So raise a glass to paths unclear,
For life's an art, both grand and dear.
In every turn, a story flows,
In divergent ways, connection grows.

Navigating the Infinite

Stars above in endless night,
Guide our hearts to boundless light.
Infinite realms beneath the sky,
Where questions roam and thoughts fly high.

Through cosmic seas, our spirits sail,
Chasing dreams on every trail.
In the silence, wisdom calls,
As the universe gently sprawls.

Maps uncharted, yet we roam,
Finding solace, calling it home.
Each discovery ignites the flame,
Of timeless wonders, never the same.

So let us chart this vast expanse,
In every heartbeat, we shall dance.
To navigate the great unknown,
Is to embrace the seeds we've sown.

The Color of Dreams Yet Unwalked

In twilight's hue, a path unfolds,
A whisper soft, in silence told.
Each step a brush, each breath a stroke,
In colors bright, our dreams bespoke.

A canvas vast, unexplored land,
With hope in heart, we take our stand.
The stars alight in skies of blue,
A tapestry of what is true.

With echoes of tomorrow near,
We chase the dawn, we conquer fear.
In every shade, a story lies,
Awakening dreams beneath the skies.

So take my hand, let's walk this way,
In hues of night that greet the day.
The color of dreams yet unwalked,
In every sigh, our spirits talked.

Journey Through the Unknown

Amidst the mist, a path unclear,
We tread with hope, we shed our fear.
With every step, the shadows dance,
An open heart, a daring chance.

Each turn reveals a hidden door,
An unmarked road, forevermore.
Through valleys deep and mountains high,
We seek the truth beneath the sky.

In whispers soft, the wind will guide,
Through tangled woods where dreams reside.
With courage bold, we forge ahead,
In the embrace of words unsaid.

A journey vast, yet ours to claim,
In the unknown, we spark our flame.
With open eyes and minds awake,
We find the path we dare to take.

Threads of Time and Tides

In currents swift, the threads shall weave,
The moments lost, the hearts believe.
With every tide, a tale unfurls,
In the fabric of our fleeting worlds.

A stitch of joy, a tear of pain,
The fibers strong, yet soft like rain.
We gather memories, threads of gold,
In the tapestry of life we hold.

From dusk to dawn, in silent rhyme,
We dance with echoes, threads of time.
A symphony of life's embrace,
In every strand, we find our place.

So let us stitch with love and light,
Through every dark, we'll find the bright.
With threads interlaced, our hearts entwined,
In the weave of time, our dreams aligned.

The Melody of Every Step

In every footfall, a song is born,
A rhythm strong, in silence worn.
With echoes sweet, the earth will hum,
The melody of where we're from.

Through paths of stone and grassy fields,
The heart reveals what time conceals.
With every note, a journey starts,
In every step, we make our marks.

A dance of footsteps, soft and light,
Through shadows cast by pale moonlight.
With every sound, a tale is spun,
The journey flows like setting sun.

So let us walk with hearts aglow,
In harmony, through high and low.
The melody of every step,
In perfect tune, where dreams are kept.

The Little Print of Every Step

Each footfall whispers soft and low,
A trace of dreams where shadows grow.
In every stride, a story we weave,
The paths we choose, the hearts we grieve.

Tiny moments, marked in sand,
Silent echoes, lives unplanned.
With every step, the journey calls,
A dance of joy before it falls.

We leave behind what cannot stay,
In tiny prints that fade away.
Yet in the dust, our laughter sings,
A tapestry of little things.

So take your steps with gentle grace,
And cherish every sacred space.
For though the trail might wind and bend,
Each little print leads to the end.

Floating on the Breeze of Tomorrow

Whispers of hope drift on the air,
Carried gently, without a care.
Tomorrow's light, a promise bright,
Floating softly, beyond our sight.

Clouds of dreams in pastel hues,
Dance above in the morning dews.
Each breath we take, a chance to soar,
With every heartbeat, we seek more.

Moments linger, escapades tease,
Future beckons like swaying trees.
Onward we glide, with hearts so free,
Bound by nothing, just you and me.

In the embrace of winds untamed,
We chase the skies, unashamed.
Floating on, through night and day,
Tomorrow's promise leads the way.

The Road that Never Ends

Winding paths through woods and glades,
Each twist and turn, a new cascade.
Leaves crunch softly beneath our feet,
The road ahead, a steady beat.

Sunset glows, a fiery hue,
A guide to places, yet untrue.
Through valleys deep and mountains tall,
We journey on, we heed the call.

Here in the dusk, dreams intertwine,
Every mile, a story divine.
With stars above, we press ahead,
The road unspoiled, where souls are led.

Though shadows grow, and fears may rise,
We find our way under vast skies.
Embracing the unknowns we see,
The road that never ends is free.

The Search for Meaning Unspooled

Threads of thought weave through the night,
In search of truth, of inner light.
Questions linger, shadows trace,
As we embark on this endless race.

Whispers echo from distant stars,
Guiding us through our silent scars.
Footsteps falter, but never cease,
In tangled moments, we find peace.

The puzzle grows, each piece reveals,
The heart's desire, what it feels.
With every turn, the fabric bends,
Unraveling as the journey blends.

Through winding roads and whispers soft,
We seek the meaning, lifting aloft.
In every heartbeat, a story told,
The search for meaning, forever bold.

When Horizons Call

In twilight's glow, the colors dance,
Whispers of dreams in a fleeting chance.
From shores unknown, I hear the sound,
A call to the skies where hopes abound.

Mountains rise with stories old,
Of journeys past and futures bold.
With every step, the heart takes flight,
Chasing the stars that pierce the night.

The ocean's song, a timeless tune,
Beneath the gaze of a silver moon.
Horizons beckon with secrets vast,
I sail on winds, unbound, steadfast.

As dawn breaks light on the waiting shore,
I tread the path to discover more.
With open arms, the world unfolds,
A canvas painted with tales retold.

A Thousand Unwritten Pages

In the quiet of night, dreams take flight,
A thousand pages, blank and bright.
With whispers of ink, the stories start,
Each word a journey, each line a heart.

Ink spills like stars on the darkened quest,
Where hopes reside and passions rest.
With courage born from the silent pen,
I write of losses, I write of when.

Moments captured in fragile light,
Echoes of laughter, shadows of fright.
Each sentence a promise, a chance to grow,
In realms of wonder, where wild dreams flow.

So let the chapters unfold each day,
In the book of life, I find my way.
With every heartbeat, a tale is spun,
A thousand pages, yet to be done.

Threads of Wandering Hearts

In the tapestry of night, hearts entwine,
Threads of longing, a delicate line.
With every whisper, a story weaves,
Wandering souls, in dreams, believe.

Across the valleys and rivers wide,
We chase the dusk, where shadows hide.
Every heartbeat is a step, a start,
In the dance of fate, two wandering hearts.

With each sunset, the stars will guide,
Paths illuminated, fears set aside.
In the fabric of time, our fates align,
Tracing the patterns where love will shine.

So let the winds carry our silent vows,
In the garden of dusk, beneath the boughs.
Threads of hope in the twilight's embrace,
Wandering hearts find their destined place.

Cascades of Longing

The waterfall whispers, secrets it keeps,
In cascades of longing, the heart gently weeps.
With every drop, a memory flows,
Echoing dreams where the wild wind blows.

In the shadows of trees, I hear the song,
Of wishes unspoken, of where we belong.
Amidst the mist, our laughter rings,
In the heart of the forest, the joy it brings.

Mountains loom like guardians tall,
While rivers of time silently call.
In every reflection, there's a piece of grace,
In the dance of water, we find our place.

So let the cascades wash over fears,
Turning my laughter into healing tears.
In nature's embrace, our spirits soar,
In the cascades of longing, forevermore.

Milton Keynes UK
Ingram Content Group UK Ltd.
UKHW022143111124
451073UK00007B/176

9 789916 907689